# ALLIGATOR
# in the
# ELEVATOR

**by Rick Charette**

**illustrated by Heidi Stetson Mario**

**Pine Point Publishing**
Rt 115, Windham, ME 04062 PINE POINT

**Pine Point Publishing**
**P.O. Box 901, Windham, Maine 04062**

**The text for this book is set in 18 point Arrus Black Bold Type.**
**The illustrations were done in colored pencil.**

**ISBN 1-884210-23-6   (soft cover)**


**Library Of Congress Catalog Card Number: 97-76200**



**Printed in the U.S.A.**
**WOZ   10 9 8 7 6 5 4 3 2 1**

For Jacob
- R.C.

For Tom, Katie, Emily and Andrew
- H.S.M.

There's an alligator in the elevator.
I can't believe what I see.

There's an alligator in the elevator
and it's making eyes at me.

"Alligator, please push number one.

I'm going up to the first floor.
Would you care to join me for some fun?"

There's an alligator in the elevator.
I can't believe what I see.

There's an alligator in the elevator
and it's making eyes at me.

"Alligator, please push number two.

I'm going up to the second floor.
Gee, I'd like to make friends with you."

There's an alligator in the elevator.
I can't believe what I see.

There's an alligator in the elevator
and it's making eyes at me.

" **Alligator, please push number three.**

I'm going up to the third floor.
Would you care to have some lunch with me?"

There's an alligator in the elevator.
I can't believe what I see.

There's an alligator in the elevator
and it's making eyes at me.

"Alligator, please push number four.
I'm going up to the fourth floor.

Tell me, what are your big teeth for?"

There's an alligator in the elevator.
I can't believe what I see.

There's an alligator in the elevator
and it's making eyes at me.

"Alligator, please push number five.

I'm going up to the fifth floor.
And I'd like to make it there alive."

There's an alligator in the elevator.
I can't believe what I see.

There's an alligator in the elevator
and it's making eyes at me.

# Alligator In The Elevator

Words & Music by Rick Charette

3. "Alligator, please push number three.
   I'm going up to the third floor.
   Would you care to have some lunch with me?"

   Chorus:

4. "Alligator, please push number four.
   I'm going up to the fourth floor.
   Tell me what are your big teeth for?"

   Chorus:

5. "Alligator, please push number five.
   I'm going up to the fifth floor.
   And I'd like to make it there alive."

   Chorus:          There's an alligator in the elevator.
                    I can't believe what I see.
                    There's an alligator in the elevator.
                    And it's making eyes at me.

One day, I was doing errands with my son Jacob who was only two and a half years old. I needed to go up to the fifth floor at the University of Maine and to save time, I thought that we would take the elevator instead of using the stairs.

When I told my son we were going to take the elevator, I noticed a look of terror come over his face as he looked up at me and said: "I don't want to go in the alligator." Of course, once he realized what an elevator was, he got very excited, especially about pushing the buttons.

As we were riding home in the car, the idea of "an alligator in the elevator" popped into my head and both of us started singing. And that's how the song originated.

As you sing along, try doing some of the motions and sign language.

During the chorus, each time the word "alligator" is sung, form alligator jaws by using your hands and arms and clapping them together two times.

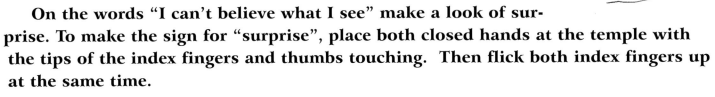 On the words "I can't believe what I see" make a look of surprise. To make the sign for "surprise", place both closed hands at the temple with the tips of the index fingers and thumbs touching. Then flick both index fingers up at the same time.

On the words "making eyes at me", form circles with your thumbs and index fingers; bring them up to your eyes as if you were looking through a pair of binoculars.

Hold up the correct number of fingers each time a floor number is mentioned.

Invent some of your own motions. Make up additional verses.

In actuality, an alligator is a powerful and dangerous animal.  Here are some interesting facts about real alligators.

# American Alligator

Do you know that: The American alligator is a large lizard-shaped reptile with four short legs and a long muscular tail. Their hide is rough and scaled. They range from 8 to 11 feet long.  The tail is about half the length of the entire body.  Males are somewhat larger than females. They may weigh more than half a ton.

The American alligator's life span ranges an average of 30 to 35 years in the wild and approximately 50 years when in captivity.

The American alligator can be found in swamps and waterways from North Carolina to the Florida Keys and west to central Texas.

The American alligator has a large stomach.  It eats fish, snakes, frogs, turtles, birds and mammals such as muskrats, deer and cows.

The American alligator's eyes, ears and nose can peek just above the water's surface in search of prey while it's body remains submerged and out-of-sight.

The American alligator has approximately 75 to 80 teeth in their mouth at one time.  When they wear down, new teeth grow to replace the old teeth.  An alligator can go through over 3000 teeth in their lifetime.  That's a lot of teeth!

The American alligator used to be listed as endangered but in recent years they are one of the few animals to be downlisted to threatened.